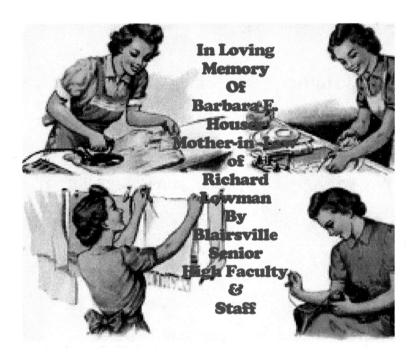

In Loving
Memory
Of
Barbara E.
House,
Mother-in-law
of
Richard
Lowman
By
Blairsville
Senior
High Faculty
&
Staff

CAREERS INSIDE THE WORLD OF

Homemaking and Parenting

A loving home produces a new generation of adults ready to enjoy life.

CAREERS & OPPORTUNITIES

CAREERS INSIDE THE WORLD OF

Homemaking and Parenting

by Maryann Miller

T 32617

B

GLOBE FEARON

Pearson Learning Group

Published in 1995, 1998 by The Rosen Publishing Group, Inc.
29 East 21st Street, New York,, New York 10010

Revised Edition 1998

Manufactured in the United States of America

ISBN 0130235350

4 5 6 7 8 9 10   05 04

Contents

INTRODUCTION

"*I* *think I want to start an Internet company,*" *Nicole told her best friend as they sat in a patch of sunshine on a bench in Central Park. "I would be the CEO, and maybe I'd be famous. You know, like Bill Gates. Except that I'm a girl.*"

"*That sounds cool,*" *replied Darcy, throwing the remnants of her cookie dough ice cream cone into the trash can. "But I think there's more to life than fame. I'm pretty sure I'm going to be a mom and run my household. It could be kind of like a company.*"

"*What?* That's *not a career! You have to work. You know, leave in the morning and get a paycheck at the end of the week,*" *said Nicole, thunderstruck.*

"*I disagree,*" *Darcy said, looking at the rollerbladers gliding by. "Why does it have to be about that? Just because all the people they had at career day worked in business or law or medicine or whatever, doesn't mean I have to. It doesn't have to be about a big paycheck.*"

"*Don't you want to be something?*" *asked Nicole. "I want to give something big back to this world. Leave my mark, be someone important.*"

"I think my mom is the most important person in the world. She raised my brother and me, and she did a good job," Darcy said with conviction. "She's worked so hard to keep my family together over the past fifteen years. She's exhausted at the end of every day, but she seems really happy. I want to be like that."

"I guess you're right," replied Nicole, squinting into the sun. "Homemaking and parenting are important jobs."

That's what this book is about—homemaking and parenting as a career. A lot of people believe that being a housewife or a househusband is the opposite of having a career. People have done it for years without even giving *themselves* credit for having a full-time job.

But it *is* a full-time job. And it can be far more challenging and rewarding than other jobs outside of the home. After all, the home that we live in and the people that we share it with are probably the most important things in our lives.

There are some obvious differences between being a homemaker and being a salesperson or a doctor or running a business. First of all, you don't get paid for raising your own children and running your own house. (But you can get paid for doing these jobs for other people, a topic that will be covered later on). But there are people, like

Homemaking and parenting careers are both difficult and rewarding.

Darcy, who think the importance of some jobs can't be measured by a simple paycheck.

A healthy family life provides young people with the equipment they need to make it in a tough world. A loving, well-adjusted home environment creates the kind of strength and security people need to become healthy adults.

The careers of parenting and homemaking do have some things in common with other careers. You have to face responsibilities, demands, and deadlines. People count on you to do your job, and meeting those challenges can be very satisfying.

This book will introduce you to all of these opportunities and help you decide if this is a career you would like to consider.

Questions to Ask Yourself

It's important to consider homemaking and parenting as serious careers. They are very different from anything else you might choose to do. 1) What makes the careers of homemaking and parenting different from other kinds of careers? 2) How are they similar to other careers? 3) What do you find most appealing about the careers of homemaking and parenting?

CHAPTER 1

WHAT IS THIS JOB?

Sarah was baby-sitting for the children of her older sister, Cheryl. Sarah baby-sat often, and she got along well with her little niece and nephew. Usually they were all dressed for bed when she got there, so it was never a big deal. But tonight her sister was late for a party, and she asked Sarah to give them dinner and bathe them before bed.

"Don't worry, Sarah," her sister told her, "You'll do fine. There are leftovers in the fridge. Just throw the casserole into the microwave. Then get them into the bath. It'll be fine. They love you!" she said as she ran out the door.

Sarah led the kids into the kitchen and found the macaroni and cheese hidden in the fridge. Melissa, the four-year old, stuck out her tongue when she saw the dish. "What's wrong Meliss? You don't like mac-n-cheese?" she asked her niece. "Yuck, yuck, yuck!" she yelled. "Me no want that. Want ice cream!" Sarah

10

Baby-sitting can be a good start on your career as a homemaker.

had never seen Melissa throw a tantrum before, but Cheryl had told her what they were like, and the little girl's face was turning bright red the way she had described. Sarah began to panic. She opened the fridge and peered inside. "Melissa want pizza?" she cooed to her niece. "Yummy!" Melissa shouted, the signs of hysteria melting away. Sarah sighed with relief.

Bath time went off without a hitch. After Melissa and her brother were dry and in their pajamas, Sarah snuggled with them on the couch. They had made her read their favorite story twice, but Sarah didn't mind. She felt warm and happy next to them. She wondered what it would be like to do this all the time. It was an interesting thought.

11

Men are taking a more active role in homemaking and parenting.

An experience like Sarah's can lead some people to consider a career as a homemaker or a parent. It may even be the way most of our parents thought about it. What is different for Sarah is that she will have more of a choice in the matter than many of our parents did.

Until around the 1970s, the role of homemaker was usually filled by a woman. The husband went to work, and the wife stayed home. If the couple had children, the wife usually was the sole caretaker.

Since women have recently reentered the work force in large numbers, men have had to take a more active role in homemaking and parenting. Even dads who don't stay home all the time are more involved in child care. They help in the evenings and on weekends. Some men even take leave from their jobs to help with a new baby. Companies now offer family leave so that men and women can take care of children together. A law was passed by the Clinton administration to ensure this opportunity for every family in America. It is called the Family and Medical Leave Act.

As more men are becoming active participants in parenting, they are discovering how rewarding it is.

But homemaking and parenting are multifaceted jobs. Couples without children and single people are still homemakers—they have to take care of the place where they live.

Overlap

People with children, whether they are a single mom or dad or a married couple living together, are both homemakers and parents. They have a lot more responsibility than people who don't have children. Many of the tasks they must perform to keep their children healthy and happy are considered homemaking tasks, like fixing dinner for their kids or cleaning their children's clothes. But these responsibilities are doubled for parents. They have twice as many dishes and twice as much wash as people without children. (More than that if they have more than one child!)

Shopping, paying bills, and maintenance are other tasks that are required for the upkeep of a home without children. But in homes with children these tasks take more time. There are more bills (kids are expensive), more things to buy, and more things to fix.

Basically, homemakers without children have to clean, cook, shop, pay bills, do errands, make appointments, and generally make sure their homes run smoothly. Those who are both homemakers and parents do those tasks, but they do

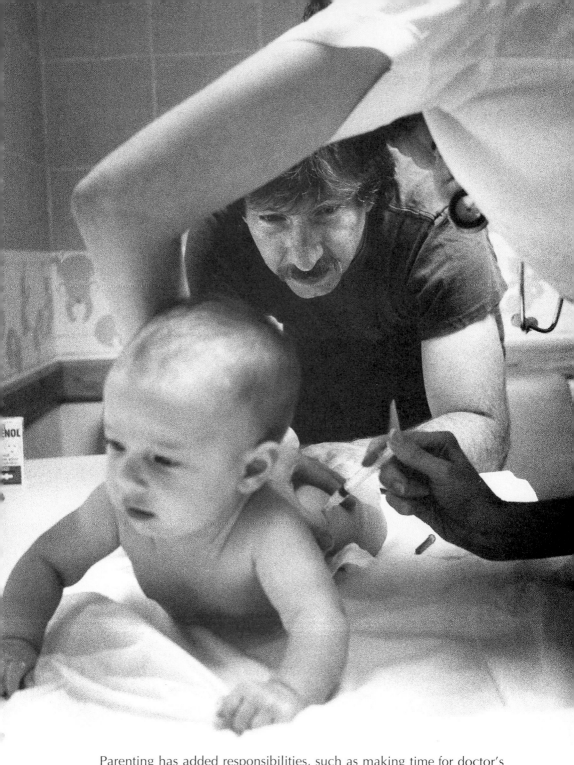

Parenting has added responsibilities, such as making time for doctor's appointments.

all these things for their kids, too. In addition, they must attend to the following children's needs:

Physical Care—nursing, feeding, clothing, bathing, doctor's visits, etc.

Emotional Care—talking, playing, teaching, reading, guiding, and loving.

Time demands—appointments, school functions, sports, other activities like dance and piano lessons, transportation, etc.

We will look at each of these areas in more detail throughout the book.

Questions to Ask Yourself

The idea of creating a home for someone can be very appealing, but also intimidating. 1) What is the difference between homemaking and parenting? 2) How have the roles of men and women changed in homemaking and parenting? 3) What are some movies or TV shows that show men in traditionally women's roles?

CHAPTER 2

PREPARING FOR YOUR CAREER

Despite the fact that parenting and homemaking are very important jobs, little formal education has been offered to teach people expertise in these fields. Most people learned from their own parents, and historically, girls would take homemaking courses in high school.

Most courses lasted only one semester, which made it difficult to learn much about being a homemaker or parent. "All I can remember is making cookies and sewing an apron," one woman said about her class in the '60s.

The good news is that high school homemaking courses have changed. Some of them introduce students to child care, family problem-solving, and financial management.

College courses have changed, too. Instead of focusing on just the basics of cooking, sewing,

There are now college courses in Child Development and Parenting.

and decorating, they cover such courses as Child Development, Parenting, and Relationships.

Another major change in homemaking courses is that they are no longer primarily for girls. Boys in most junior high schools are required to take home economics.

Other courses are available to prepare you for the role of homemaker or parent or both:

Parenting. Take child psychology courses in high school and college. General psychology and sociology are also useful.

Some colleges offer continuing education courses in parenting. Similar programs are also offered through schools and houses of worship.

Homemaking. Time-management courses are helpful for planning and efficiency. Handling family finances becomes easier after taking some money-management classes. Courses in repairs and home maintenance are usually available through continuing education or recreation programs.

Educate Yourself

As we've discussed, homemaking and parenting are both huge responsibilities. Many people who do have babies are not yet ready. This is one of the reasons why we have so many single-parent families.

Although many men take on the responsibilities of fatherhood, there are far more single mothers raising children than single fathers. Single moms also have it tough because men often make higher wages than women do. Often, when young women have unplanned pregnancies, they drop out of school. It's much harder to get a high school or college diploma when you are raising a young child. There isn't a lot of extra time for studying. We will talk more about these issues later on.

Go to the Source

Another way to find out more about homemaking

and child care is to talk to people who are doing the jobs. Your own parents would be a good first source. Then talk to young parents, single parents, and people who have no children. Ask them how they handle their responsibilities.

Some other good questions to ask are:

- What are the best things about being a homemaker/parent?
- What are the worst things?
- Did you manage another career in addition to homemaking/parenting? How did you do it?
- Did you take time away from another career to be a full-time homemaker/parent? What are the advantages and disadvantages of doing that?
- What are the most important things to consider in deciding to have child?

Keep in mind that both careers are full of surprises. The ability to be flexible and adapt to the unexpected will give you a better chance for success.

Questions to Ask Yourself

Neither homemaking nor parenting is an easy job. Both require a lot of preparation and common sense. 1) What courses can you take in school to

Parents are always learning about their career, from other parents and from people who have no children.

help you prepare for a career in homemaking or parenting? 2) What can you do on your own to help you prepare for a career in homemaking or parenting? 3) Whom can you talk to in order to learn more about homemaking and parenting?

CHAPTER 3

A DAY IN THE LIFE OF A HOMEMAKER

If your mom is a full-time homemaker, have you ever thought about what she does all day? Do the clean clothes magically appear in your room every week? What happens to the dust in the living room? Who pays the bills so the lights don't get turned off?

You may think those questions are silly. But some young people haven't been actively involved in housekeeping with their parents, so they don't know what is involved.

The following are the basic responsibilities:

Cleaning. Routine jobs like dusting, vacuuming, cleaning the bathroom, sweeping, cleaning appliances, washing dishes. Also periodic jobs like washing windows, cleaning closets, washing curtains, shampooing carpeting and furniture, cleaning walls and baseboards.

Laundry. Sorting, washing, drying, folding,

Homemaking is not an easy task.

and putting away clothes. Taking other clothes to the cleaners and picking them up.

Shopping. Planning meals and making a list of items needed. Taking an inventory of other items needed such as paper products and soap products. Going to the store, then putting everything away.

Cooking. Preparing meals that meet nutritional needs; preparing for special occasions such as holidays and guests.

Maintenance/yardwork. Home repairs, painting, lawn mowing, trimming, edging, watering, weeding, planting, clean-up.

Financial. Planning a budget, paying bills, handling insurance, investments, and savings.

Seeing it all listed together like that is almost enough to make you want to run for cover. That's an awful lot of work! How would I manage it?

The Dreaded "O" Word

The key to getting jobs done in any career is *organization*. A person has to come up with a plan to get things done and meet deadlines. It is the same with homemaking.

People who accomplish a lot make a plan for the jobs. In *Sidetracked Home Executives*, Pam Young and Peggy Jones offer a detailed plan. They suggest looking at each room and writing down what has to be done, then assigning each job a time. For instance:

BEDROOM
    Make bed—daily
    Dust—weekly
    Vacuum—weekly
    Change sheets—weekly
    Clean drawers and closets—monthly
    Wash windows—monthly
    Clean cobwebs—monthly

Make a similar list of jobs for each room of the house. Then the authors suggest writing the

Homemaking often involves a lot of cooking.

jobs on index cards and filing them according to when the job should be done. Each day do the daily jobs, then pick some from the weekly and monthly files to do.

This is a good plan, but not everybody likes that kind of organization.

Marie keeps her house clean by having a weekly cleaning session. Everybody in the family participates. Marie makes a list of jobs, and each person chooses one. As jobs are finished, others are chosen until all the jobs are done.

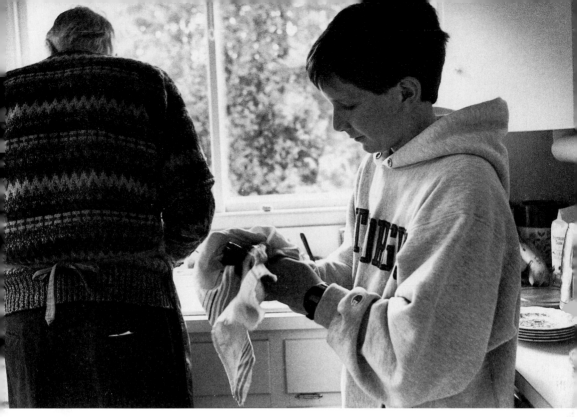
Taking care of a home can be a family team effort.

Everyone is responsible for making their own bed. The other daily chores are done on a rotating basis. Most of the time, Marie and her husband take turns cooking.

"We like not having a strict plan we have to follow," Marie says. "It lets us schedule the jobs around our activities and interests. I think our approach also works because everyone is involved. Nobody can whine and say they do more than the rest of the family."

Marie has another job outside the home, but her approach is shared by a full-time homemaker in Colorado. "I told my family if there are six people messing up a house it shouldn't be one person's

27

responsibility to clean it up," Cleo says. Everyone in Cleo's family cleans their own room. Meal preparation and clean-up are a team effort, and everyone helps with the laundry. Larger cleaning jobs are also a group effort, including yardwork. "This is a great arrangement for a family," Cleo says. "It gets the work done, and we spend more time together. Sometimes it's more fun than work."

The Upside

Being a full-time homemaker has a number of advantages. You decide how and when things will be done. Having that kind of control over your job can be very satisfying. It gives you freedom that you don't have in other positions.

Questions to Ask Yourself

Just like every other career, there are certain responsibilities and tricks to being successful in homemaking and parenting. It's important to know what these are before starting on your career. 1) What are some basic responsibilities of housekeeping? 2) What is the key to getting jobs done in any career? 3) What are some advantages of being a full-time homemaker?

CHAPTER 4

PARENTING: THE CHALLENGES AND REWARDS

Family is no longer defined as it was in the 1950s. The concept of the "nuclear" family—a unit comprised of a mother, father, and two children—has disappeared along with rotary phones and eight-track tapes. Today we have single-parent families (with either mothers or fathers as heads of households), blended families, and families with no children. There are foster families. There are children who live with adoptive families and don't know their birth parents. There are families with two parents of the same sex, who are sometimes called domestic partners.

The divorce rate has increased dramatically over the last few years, which accounts for the ever-growing number of single parent homes. The role of the single parent is especially hard. As mentioned in an earlier chapter, it is much more difficult for single parents to endure the expenses

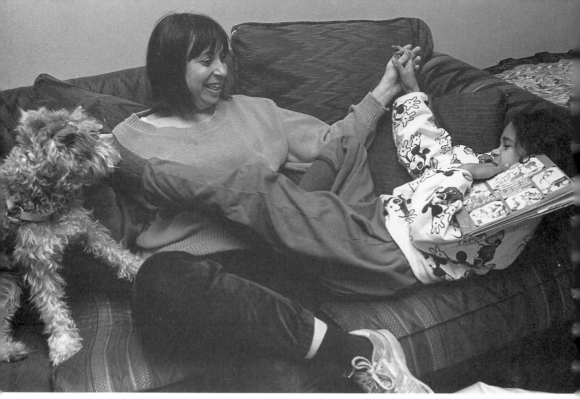
A high divorce rate has increased the number of single-parent families.

of child care and homemaking. They often have to work another full-time job and must pay for day care or baby-sitters. Single mothers are also often the object of ridicule and blame by the media. When a child raised by a single mom acts out or gets into trouble, people often target the mother as the responsible party. This is grossly unfair, because a single parent has to work twice as hard as anyone else raising a child.

The success of parenting in any situation requires a commitment of time and self. Each parent has to answer the question, "How much of myself am I willing to invest in family life?"

Responsibilities

Parents have to take care of the physical and emotional needs of their children. Most parents find the physical needs easier to meet. Those needs include feeding, clothing, providing a home and transportation, and educational and medical considerations.

Meeting those needs can be physically tiring, but they are less challenging than the emotional needs of children.

It sounds easy, but to achieve that goal a parent must help the child attain:

- Independence
- Responsibility
- Emotional stability
- Confidence
- Self-control

Parents do this by satisfying the basic emotional needs of their children:

Love—Children need to know that they are important and someone cares for them. They should be loved and appreciated for who they are, not what they do. This builds self-esteem and confidence.

Security—Children need to believe that someone will take care of their physical and emotional needs. They also need to know that someone will protect them from harm. They need to feel safe.

Continuity—Children need things they can

count on. Some of those things include routines, traditions, holiday celebrations, and time spent together on a regular basis. They also need to know what they can and cannot do, as well as what is expected of them.

Communication—Children need to be heard. They need to know that their ideas and concerns are important. They need to talk to someone who understands and accepts them no matter what outrageous things they say.

Identity—Children need to feel proud of who they are. They also need to be encouraged to find their individual gifts and talents.

Belonging—Children need to feel that they are part of a group that can provide support and guidance. This need can first be met by the family, but it extends outside the home. Parents can encourage their children to join school or community organizations.

Respect—Children need to be treated with respect. This helps them to feel secure in their identity and also teaches them respect for others.

Parents who strive to provide their children with these emotional needs create a foundation that will last a lifetime.

Jamie is a single mother with two children. Tommy is four years old and Carly has just started

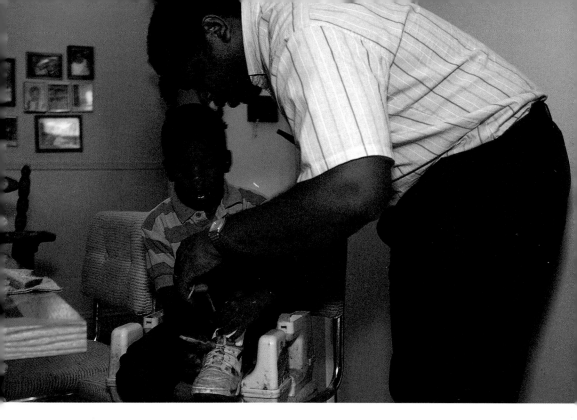

Children need to feel security.

her "terrible twos." Jamie's ex-husband has long since stopped providing any emotional support to her and the kids—he only gives her what money he must provide by law. Tommy is old enough to notice that his daddy doesn't live with his family like other boys' daddies do, and he is starting to ask questions and feel different.

Jamie had anticipated the struggle Tommy would have coming to terms with the absence of his father, and she bought books on children of divorce. She also talked to some of her adult friends who came from single-parent homes. She asked her boss at the advertising agency if she could start

33

working from home, and she now conducts her business as a "telecommuter" so she can be home during the day.

When Tommy comes home from kindergarten each weekday afternoon, Jamie makes sure she has already given enough quality time to Carly, so that the little girl will nap peacefully and she can give all of her energy to her son. Tommy sometimes asks Jamie if she will leave him like Daddy did. She tells him that Daddy didn't leave because Tommy was a bad boy, and his dad still loves him although he doesn't live with them.

All her work has paid off: Tommy is becoming a well-adjusted, confident child, and stability is at the center of their home. Jamie knows it won't be easy, but she is certain that both her children will grow up believing in themselves.

Love Often Means Laying Down the Law

If you want your children to grow up whole and happy, you should create a home in which they know that they have responsibilities, too. Giving lots of love doesn't mean giving them everything they want all the time. There are several styles of discipline that parents choose:

Authoritarian—Parents have the most power. They dictate what children will do.

How parents discipline a child depends on their parenting style.

Permissive—Children have the most power. They dictate what they will do and sometimes what the parent will do.

Authoritative—Parents have ultimate power, but children are part of the decision-making process.

Of these, the authoritative style is the most desirable. Experts agree that families need rules and children need guidance and mutual respect.

The whole point of discipline is to set limits. This can be done through education, example, encouragement, cooperation, and firmness.

35

Family and Work

Many parents face the question of who will be the primary caregiver for the children. More women today work outside the home than ever before. That raises concerns about childcare and who carries the load at home.

Some people believe that one parent should stay at home with the children all the time, and most experts agree that it is very important for at least the first year. That should always be taken into consideration in making the decision about work.

But more often than not there is no real choice in the matter. Survival often dictates that both parents work. Many parents do not have an option. What do you do then?

You make the best decision you can about day care, baby-sitters, and after-school programs. Some large corporations and small businesses are creating excellent day-care facilities to accommodate parents and their children. This way, moms and dads can visit their kids on their lunch break. If you work outside of the home and your company doesn't offer that option, visit as many day-care facilities in your neighborhood as you can, and interview baby-sitters. Don't forget to check their references. Talk to teachers and administrators. Talk to the children and their parents.

Many parents share care of the kids.

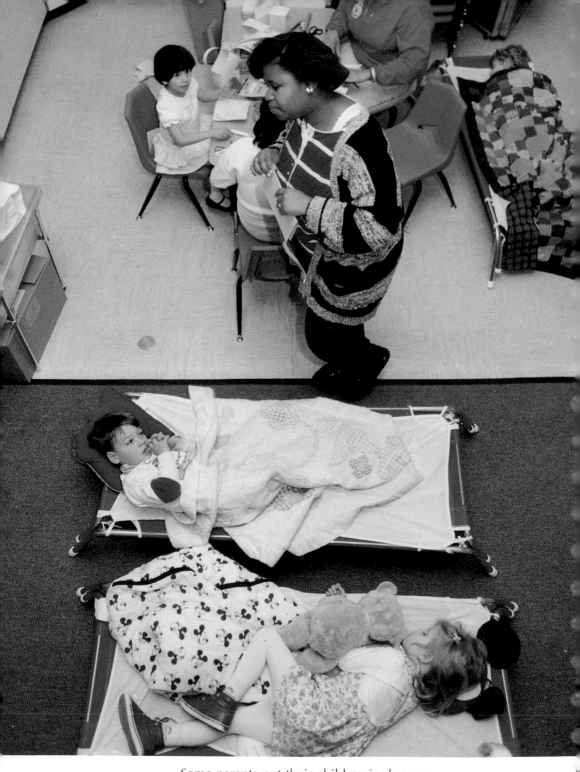

Some parents put their children in day care.

Let your children visit day-care facilities and meet baby-sitters in advance. Children have strong intuitions. If they feel uncomfortable in a situation, there is probably something wrong.

Questions to Ask Yourself

Parents have to make many difficult choices about the upbringing of their child. No one way is perfect; however, there is usually one way that is best for your family. 1) Do you have the coping tools necessary to provide your kids with the emotional stability they need? 2) What style of parenting do you think is best? Why? 3) Would you want to work outside the home? Why or why not?

CHAPTER 5

ARE YOU REALLY READY?

Elisa and Mike have been dating since they were fourteen. Now that they are about to start their senior year, they are talking about what will happen when they graduate. "Mike, you know I want to go to the state school. They have an excellent psychology program and besides, a bunch of my friends are going. I think it would be a great experience for me," Elisa said. Mike isn't so sure about that. He plans to start work at his father's framing business as soon as he graduates and he wants Elisa to go to the community college so they can stay together.

Tonight they went to a party, and their friend Charlene mentioned something about next year. An argument flared up between Mike and Elisa. Elisa is torn between her feelings for her boyfriend and her plans for college. She can see herself marrying him and starting a family, but she is afraid that she'll never become a psychologist if she commits to a family now. Besides, her parents are encouraging her to go to the state school, because her grades and SAT scores are high. But who knows what will happen if she waits and tries to apply again in a few years?

You spend a tremendous amount of emotional energy when you're considering the commitment to becoming a parent or a homemaker. It's not the kind of job you can back out of like working at a bank. Once you have children, you can't return them to the store like a shirt that doesn't fit. So, are you ready now?

The dropout rate for high school students has increased dramatically over the last few years. Much of this is due to unplanned pregnancies. Once you have the responsibility of a child, going back to school to get your degree will be harder than it is right now. Planning is essential; getting a good job, if you intend to work outside of the home, is almost impossible without at least a high school diploma.

Making the Decision

Even those people who plan to finish high school and maybe go to college or graduate school, like Elisa, have to make careful and detailed plans. Lists are an essential ingredient for any planning session. Whatever career you are considering, it helps to visualize the pros and cons.

HOMEMAKING

Good Points	Bad Points
Be own boss	Work is never done
Set own hours	Unplanned interruptions
Choose what jobs to do when	Role not valued by others

PARENTING

Good Points	Bad Points
Experience the miracle of life	Constant demands
Have someone else to love	Getting up at night
Pride in what child accomplishes	Disappointments
Sharing good times	Unexpected emergencies
Growing in friendship	Conflict

Some other questions you might ask yourself are: Do I like to cook and clean? Do I enjoy babies and children? Do I get frustrated easily? Do I mind sharing?

Learning to Budget Time and Money

If you decide to commit to this career, you will have to learn some techniques for time management and budgeting. You won't have a boss coming into your office to tell you that there's a meeting to feed the baby at 3:00 that you have to attend. You'll have to figure out when and how to do everything to run your home well. Some of this will come from experience, but there are ways that you can prepare.

Remember that this is not a paying job. You will have to make sure there is a source of income supporting your home, because babies are expensive. Can you work from home? Do you have a partner who will work full time to support the family while you act as the homemaker? Can you take your children to your place of work?

If you've figured out how to support your family, the next step is making sure you don't overspend. Creating a budget is a vital first step toward making money last throughout the week. Take out a notebook and write down how much income you have. Then make a list of everything you need for your home and family. Make sure you have enough money for the basic necessities: food, diapers, electricity, rent, cable, and the phone bill. You'll also need to know how to manage and balance a checkbook. This way, you can always know how much money you have in the bank and how much you can afford to spend.

Beyond managing your money, you'll need to figure out how to budget your time. Lists will help with this task, too. Get an organizer that has a calendar and slots for every hour of the day. You can buy one at stationery stores and drugstores. Now, think about everything you need to accomplish each week: laundry, food shopping, taking the kids to the doctor, the cat to the vet, getting the car washed, ordering a new filter for the sink, etc. Write those down in your organizer on the day you intend to get them done. This won't always happen, of course. Lists are more about intention than absolute deadlines. But it is always gratifying to cross finished tasks off the page.

When you have carefully gone through the decision-making process and decided that this career is definitely for you, you will have a lot to look forward to. The life you share with your family will be based on hard work, shared responsibility, and a lot of joy!

Questions to Ask Yourself

You're almost an adult. You'll have to carefully weigh all the pros and cons of life as a homemaker and/or parent. 1) Am I emotionally ready to commit to this career now? 2) Can I afford to do this, and can I be organized enough to manage my time? 3) Do I want to change my lifestyle into that of a homemaker and/or parent, or do I want to continue to explore other options?

CHAPTER 6

CREATING SUCCESS

The rewards for homemaking and parenting are much different from those of other careers. You don't get a paycheck. There is no bonus plan. You don't get to dress up and go to important meetings. And you don't get vacation days and sick days.

So why do it? Because it is important work. Many of our social problems can be directly linked to family problems.

Some people choose to be a homemaker or a parent or both because doing the job well can give enormous personal satisfaction. A homemaker can take great pride in creating a warm, loving environment. Parents can take great pride in seeing their children grow into mature, healthy, interesting people.

Many parents put their success in child-rearing

above all others. A successful journalist in St. Louis puts it this way: "I've done a lot in my life that some people might envy. I've worked at high-profile, high-paying jobs, known athletic success, graduated from prestigious schools. But when I think of my achievements, I don't think of these things. I think of my sons."

A father who took a leave from his other job to help raise his kids has this to say, "The six months of my personal leave were the most productive and happiest of my life. Now when I come home from work at night, I feel like a real dad, not just a visitor."

A mother makes this comment, "Although I don't receive a salary, I consider my career one of the most satisfying, fulfilling, and at times most stressful jobs in society. Homemaking is an exciting and rewarding job and should be viewed as more than a leave of absence from society."

Another journalist who was a full-time mother first puts it this way, "There are more instant and obvious rewards from being a lawyer, or an astronaut, or a business executive, and we mothers aren't often that lucky. The pay is lousy and the only notoriety we can expect is to be taken to school for show-and-tell if we have an interesting hobby. But after investing almost seventeen years in the career, I'm beginning to see the first fruits of my efforts unfolding. Believe me, it was worth the wait."

Outside Influence

Other attitudes about full-time homemaking or parenting are not always so positive. Some people still think the careers are a terrible waste of time and talent, especially for women.

Before there were equal rights for women, many of them were trapped in roles of wife and mother. Now they have more freedom of choice. Some people think women shouldn't choose domestic careers, that by doing so they are taking a step backward.

This makes it more difficult for young people who are facing choices. One teen surprised her mother by saying she wasn't sure she wanted to go to college. "Why not?" the mother asked.

"I'm not sure I ever really wanted to do that. I just thought I had to. People have been telling me to plan big things for my life. No one told me I could be a wife and mother if I want."

Your choice about your career should be based on what you really want to do, not on what someone else thinks you should do.

If you do choose parenting or homemaking, you will have to find your own rewards. How well you do this will depend on your attitude.

As a homemaker you will spend many hours cleaning a house that only gets dirty again. As a parent, you will spend endless energy raising a child who may not end up as your pride and joy.

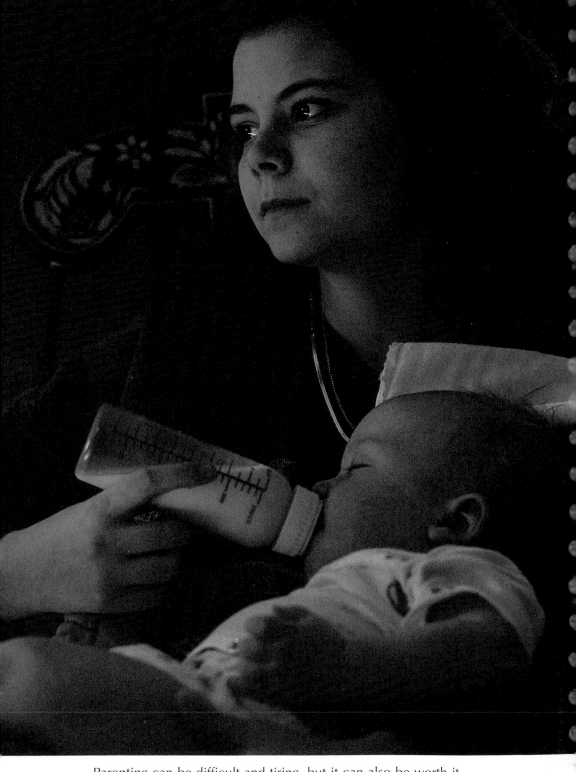

Parenting can be difficult and tiring, but it can also be worth it.

To avoid stress and burnout, psychologists recommend the following:

- Believe in yourself and your ability.
- Find something positive in your job everyday.
- Arrange time just for yourself.
- Join or start a support group.
- Maintain a sense of humor.

One mother believes that laughter is one of the best tools she has. "It can change a lot of situations," she says. "Say, for instance, you're going head to head with your thirteen-year-old son who is trying to intimidate you with his macho stance. So you turn it into a joke. You smile and tell him he is not going to get his way no matter how much he narrows his eyes and glares at you. Then you gently tease him out of his anger and pretty soon you are both laughing.

"You've still gotten your point across, and you both end up feeling good about the resolution."

The value of laughter is that it is so uplifting. It makes it easier to face the frustrations and demands of any job.

Questions to Ask Yourself

You have to make the choice of which career to follow. Think before you choose. Make sure it's *your* decision, and not anyone else's. 1) Why do you want to be a parent or homemaker? 2) What are "outside influences"? 3) How might outside influences affect your decisions in life?

CHAPTER 7

OTHER OPPORTUNITIES

You can also be a professional in these fields by working for someone else. Private Household Worker is a title given to people who provide services for other people. They generally clean homes, care for children, plan and cook meals, and do laundry.

Au pairs receive room and board in exchange for housekeeping or caring for children.

Houseworkers do only household cleaning.

Child-care workers care for children, wash their clothes, and clean their rooms.

Nannies care for young children.

Tutors or **Governesses** look after older children, help them with schoolwork, and may teach a foreign language.

Companions or **Personal attendants** care for elderly or disabled people. They help with bathing and dressing, prepare and serve meals, take them on outings and to appointments.

Homes with a large staff of household workers may include a **housekeeper** and a **butler**. They hire, supervise, and coordinate the work of the household staff. Butlers greet guests, answer phones, deliver messages, serve food and drinks. A butler may also drive the car and act as a personal attendant.

Cooks plan and prepare meals, clean the kitchen, order groceries and supplies.

Caretakers do heavy household work and general home maintenance.

Most household workers live in their own home and travel to work. The job requires no special training.

Special schools for nannies, butlers, housekeepers, and governesses teach household administration, bookkeeping, early childhood education, nutrition, and child care.

Private household workers can move into similar jobs in hospitals, hotels, and restaurants. The pay is usually better, and companies offer benefits such as medical insurance.

Most household workers work part time, less than 35 hours a week. Earnings vary from $10 an hour in a large city to minimum wage in other areas. Travel expenses to and from work are usually paid, and the worker receives a free meal.

Live-in workers earn more and receive free room and board. They also usually work longer hours and are limited in their contact with friends and relatives. In 1990 the average pay was $110 to $226 per week. The top 10 percent earned $290 a week or more.

Most live-in housekeepers or butlers, nannies, and governesses earn higher wages. Trained nannies in New York City can start at $250 to $450 per week and go as high as $800 per week.

Most private household workers have no health insurance, retirement plans, or unemployment compensation.

Child Care

Caring for other people's children is a good way to have an income and be at home with your own children. It also fills a great need.

Most people who provide at-home care earn between $3 and $5 an hour per child. The rate depends on how much care the child needs and what other services are provided. For after-school care, some people will take a child to athletic practices or other scheduled activities.

Caring for infants and toddlers at home can be very time-consuming. Some people even offer structured learning activities similar to a preschool. The charge for this is higher than for basic child care.

A person can also be licensed to run a day-

Instead of having kids of your own, you can work at a day care center.

care center at home. Each state regulates day-care centers.

Another option in day care is to work for an established center. Entry-level positions pay a little more than minimum wage. The responsibilities include watching the children during play-time and assisting the teachers.

To move into a higher-paying position requires more education and experience. In most centers, teachers have to have a degree in early education. Degrees in psychology and business would qualify you for a position as a director or manager.

Other

Some jobs in hotels and on cruise ships are related to "domestic services." A valet, for instance, assists guests with personal needs.

To work in a hotel or on a cruise ship, training is required. Universities that offer programs in hotel and restaurant management usually offer training in housekeeping and valet positions.

Questions to Ask Yourself

Sometimes paid jobs in the field of homemaking and parenting are the best option. They provide experience for later on, and also give an idea of what the field is really about. 1) What paid jobs using homemaking and parenting skills are available? 2) What kind of training is available for these jobs?

CHAPTER 8

HOW DO I START?

Get involved at home. Ask your parents to teach you more about running a household. Plan meals and shop together. Take turns cooking. Baby-sit. Take child-care classes. Work in the church nursery or at a day-care center.

Keep in mind, however, that no career choice has to be final. Many people change careers, blend careers, or start a new career.

One advantage of this career is that you have options. You can work at another career at home. You can start another career after your children are grown. Or you can plan for one by going to school.

Questions to Ask Yourself

If you think you might be interested in a career in homemaking, get a head start. 1) What is a good way to begin learning the skills? 2) What is one advantage of starting with a career in home-making or parenting?

Homemaking and parenting can be careers full of rewards.

GLOSSARY

adversities Problems, misfortune, bad luck.

authoritarian Favoring absolute obedience to authority, against individual freedom.

authoritative Coming from proper authority.

budget Plan of how to balance income and spending.

contradictory Saying the opposite of a statement; inconsistent.

dictate To issue orders or commands.

domestic Pertaining to family or home.

homemaker Person who manages a household.

parent Person who has the responsibility of raising a child.

permissive Not strict, allowing freedom to act in a manner of a child's own choosing.

APPENDIX A

The Center for Successful Fathering
13740 Research Boulevard G-4
Austin, Texas 78750
(512) 335-8106 (direct)
(800) 537-0853 (toll-free)
(512) 2588-2591 (fax)

Children Now
E-mail: children@dnai.com
(1-800) CHILD-44

Families and Work Institute
330 7th Avenue
New York, NY 10001
Web site: http://www.familiesandworkinst.org/

Mother's Matter
171 Wood Street
Rutherford, NJ 07070
(201) 933-8191

National Organization of Single Mothers
PO Box 68
Midland, NC 28107

National Parent Information Network
ERIC Clearinghouse on Elementary and Early
    Childhood Education
University of Illinois at Urbana-Champaign
Children's Research Center
51 Gerty Drive
Champaign, IL 61820-7469
(217) 333-1386 (direct)
(1-800) 583-4135 (toll-free)
(217) 333-3766 (fax)
E-mail: ericeece@uiuc.edu

Parents Helping Parents
3041 Olcott Street
Santa Clara, CA 95054-3222
(408) 727-5775 (phone)
(408) 727-0182 (fax)

Parents Without Partners International, Inc.
401 North Michigan Avenue
Chicago, IL 60611-4267
(312) 644-6610

Single Mothers by Choice
PO Box 1642
Gracie Square Station
New York, NY 10028
(212) 988-0993

APPENDIX B

Legal Rights of Parents and Children

Parents have the legal right to custody of their children. They have a duty to provide food, shelter, clothing, and medical attention until the children are of age.

Parents are also responsible for the behavior of their children. They can be held liable for harm caused by their children.

Parents have the right to the services of a child living with them, including earnings.

Children are free from legal ties to their parents when they become adults; when they enter military service; or when parent and child agree that the child is able to support himself.

Children who run away can be arrested, returned home, or placed in foster care.

Children also have legal rights. Parents cannot physically abuse or neglect their children.

Children have the right to an education. If a parent interferes with this right, authorities can take action.

FOR FURTHER READING

Azzerrad, Jacob. *Anyone Can Have a Happy Child: How to Nurture Emotional Intelligence.* New York: M. Evans & Co., 1997.

Blocker, Anne K. *Baby Basics: A Guide for New Parents.* Minnetonka, MN: Chronimed Publishers, 1997.

Einzig, Mitchell J., M.D. (ed.) *Baby & Child Emergency First-Aid Handbook: Simple Step-by-Step Instructions for the Most Common Childhood Emergencies.* Deephaven, MN: Meadowbrook Press, 1994.

Kennedy, Marge. *100 Things You Can Do to Keep Your Family Together. . .When It Sometimes Seems Like the Whole World Is Trying to Pull It Apart.* New York: Peterson's Guides, 1994.

Levine, James A. and Todd L.Pittensky. *Working Fathers: New Strategies for Combining Work and Family.* New York: Family and Work Institute, 1997.

Ramming, Cindy. *All Mothers Work: A Guilt Free Guide for the Stay-at-Home Mom.* New York: Avon Books, 1996.

Rolfe, Randy. *The 7 Secrets of Successful Parents.* Chicago, IL: Contemporary Books, 1997.

Tolliver, Cindy. *At-Home Motherhood: Making It Work for You.* San Jose, CA: Resource Publications, 1994.

INDEX

ABOUT THE AUTHOR
Maryann Miller has been published in numerous magazines and Dallas newspapers. She has served as editor, columnist, reviewer, and feature writer.

Married for over 30 years, Ms. Miller is the mother of five children. She and her husband live in Omaha, Nebraska.

PHOTO CREDITS
Cover photo © Maria Taglienti/Image Bank; pp. 2, 11, 33, 53 © Hazel Hankin/Impact Visuals; p. 8 © Michael Kamber/Impact Visuals; p. 12 © Katherine McGlynn/Impact Visuals; pp. 15, 24 © Piet van Lier/Impact Visuals; p. 18 © Evan Johnson/Impact Visuals; p. 21 h© Jane Schreibman/ Impact Visuals; p. 26 © Jim West/Impact Visuals; p. 27 © Catherine Smith/ Impact Visuals; p. 30 © Linda Eber/Impact Visuals; p. 33 © Harvey Finkle/ Impact Visuals; p. 36 © Andrew Lichtenstein/Impact Visuals; p. 37 © M. Brodskay/Impact Visuals; p. 39 © AP/Wide World Photos; p. 48 © Dick Doughty/Impact Visuals; p. 56 © Sharon Stewart/ Impact Visuals.
PHOTO RESEARCH: Vera Ahmadzadeh with Jennifer Croft
DESIGN: Kim Sonsky